"HOW TO BECOME A WONDER WOMAN?"

WITHOUT SPILLING YOUR COFFEE

SAALINI VELLIVEL

To every woman who's ever looked in the mirror and
questioned her worth,
To the girl I used to be — scared, silenced, yet quietly
brave,
To the women who raised me, stood beside me, and never
let me forget who I am,
To the late-night overthinkers, the heart-healers, the
boundary-setters, and the quiet fighters...

This book is for you.

It's for the woman who stayed soft in a world that told her
to harden.
For the one who broke, rebuilt, and still chose love.
For the one who's still searching — not for perfection, but
for peace.

May these pages remind you that power doesn't always
roar.
Sometimes, it whispers in your heart and moves through
your scars.
You are, and have always been, a Wonder Woman.

With all my love and fire,
Saalini Vellivel

Contents

Foreword

I didn't grow up feeling like a Wonder Woman.
Like many women, I often felt lost in the noise of expectations, heartbreaks, and the pressure to be "enough." I've cried quietly, doubted myself loudly, and fought invisible battles that no one saw.

This book was born out of those moments. It's not a manual from someone who has it all figured out. It's a guide from someone who's still growing, still healing, still learning — just like you.

Each page carries a piece of my truth, a lesson I've lived, and a voice I wish I had heard when I needed it most. This book is for every woman who has ever questioned her worth, swallowed her pain, or played small to make others comfortable.

You are not alone. And you are far more powerful than you've been told.

My hope is that this guide helps you reconnect with your strength, set your boundaries, love yourself fiercely, and become the Wonder Woman you were always meant to be — not perfect, but powerful in your own way.

Let's walk this journey together.
With love and fire,
Saalini Vellivel

Preface

Writing this book was one of the most healing things I've ever done.

Not because I had all the answers — but because I had all the questions. Who am I? What am I meant for? How do I become the woman I dream of being?

As I sat down to write, memories came rushing in. Painful ones. Beautiful ones. And all the lessons in between. This book became a safe space for my truth — and I hope it becomes one for yours too.

We're not here just to survive. We're here to thrive, to feel deeply, to grow, and to shine.

This book is a piece of my soul. I offer it to you with all my heart. May it guide you back to yours.

Acknowledgements

To the women who lit the path before me — your strength is the reason I could take this first step.
To my family and friends who supported me in silence and in storm — thank you for holding space for my voice.
To every woman who reads these words — you are my why.

And to the version of me who kept going, even when it hurt — this book is for you

Prologue

To the Wonder Woman Within You — This Is Your Awakening

"You don't become a Wonder Woman. You remember that you always were."

This book is not written from perfection but from the battlefield.

From the moment I stood in the shower, silently crying, and still showed up smiling the next morning.

From the nights I wore my strength like armour and hope like a secret prayer.

"I survived. I stood tall. I stayed soft."

And somewhere along the way, I became my inspiration.

But I didn't do it alone.

I rose on the strength of women who didn't even know they were lifting me.

My mother, whose silence was a sermon.

My sister, who showed me the beauty in quiet resilience.

My mother-in-law carried softness like power.

And the countless women, friends, teachers, and strangers who taught me through their survival.

"Every woman you meet is carrying an untold miracle."

This book is my thank you to them.

And now, it's for you.

Pause & Reflect:

- Who has quietly shaped your strength without ever realising it?
- What part of your past self would thank you for surviving?
- Can you name a moment when you were your own hero?

This is not a manual to become what the world expects. This is a mirror.

A mirror that says: You are not becoming—you are remembering.

Even in a world that tries to mute you...
Question you...
Shrink you...

You rise. Still. Softly. Strongly. Always.

Because women are not fragile — we are forged.
We are not weak — we are woven from storms and stardust.
And we are not here to be small — we are here to **expand.**

Say This Aloud:

- "I am not a version of someone else's dream. I am the author of my own becoming."
- "My softness is not weakness. My silence is not absence. My story is powerful."

By the time you reach the last page, I don't want you to feel transformed — I want you to feel **seen.**

Seen in your mess and your magic.
In your quiet days and your comeback nights.
In your heartbreak and your healing.

If even one part of this book feels like a hug, a mirror, or a homecoming, then I've done what I came here to do.

Because, darling...
You are already wonderful. No more proof needed.

ONE

DEFINING INNER POWER

"You were never powerless — you were just waiting to remember."

Let's begin with a truth:

You were never missing anything.

You were never broken.

You were never too weak.

You were disconnected from something that has always been there — your inner power.

This power doesn't always roar.

It doesn't always come with medals or a spotlight.

Sometimes, it's the whisper that says "You can" when fear appears ", You can't."

Sometimes, it's the courage to choose rest instead of feeling guilty.

To walk away instead of explaining.

To speak up, even if your voice trembles.

Let's pause here:

- What does **inner power** feel like in your body?
- When was the last time you said yes to yourself, even when it was hard?

Inner power isn't just about confidence.
It's about connection to your truth, your values, your intuition.
It's quiet, steady, and deeply rooted.
It shows up in small acts of bravery.
In tears held back until you're alone.
In boundaries drawn with trembling hands.
In choosing yourself, again and again.
You don't have to find your power; You just have to remember it.
Because it's already inside you — waiting for you to listen.

A Thought for You:

Every woman holds a fire.
Some let it burn quietly.
Some dim it to keep others warm.
And some — finally — give it the space to rise and light everything they touch.
Which one are you today?
I don't believe inner power arrives all at once.
It builds over time — through every phase, every fall, every rise.
It's inherited from women who endured, loved, and survived before us.
But it's also earned through heartbreak, healing, loss, growth, and everything in between.
The girl grows.
The woman rises.

And with every chapter, she gathers more of herself.

That's what this book is here to help you do.

Not to give you something new, but to help you return to what's already yours.

Your Power, Reimagined:

- A powerful woman doesn't prove — she knows.
- She doesn't chase — she attracts.
- She doesn't shrink — she sets boundaries.
- She isn't perfect — she's present.

She listens to her intuition.
She loves without losing herself.
She knows how to say "enough."
She knows how to begin again.

Journal With Me:

- What part of your inner world are you most proud of — your strength, your softness, your survival?
- When did you first realise you were more powerful than you thought?
- Think of a moment you doubted yourself but made it through anyway. What did that teach you about your resilience?
- What stories from your past shaped your belief in your strength, for better or worse?
- Do you trust your intuition? What would change in your life if you followed it more closely?

- If your inner self had a voice, what would she ask for today?

You don't need the world's permission to step into your power.
You don't need a title, a platform, or approval.
You just need one moment of remembering.
One choice is to trust yourself.
One decision to come back to your truth.
And in that moment, your life begins to shift — from the inside out.
Let this be the start.
Your power is not out there.
It's **in here**.

TWO

PERSONAL EXPERIENCES — THE BECOMING OF A WONDER WOMAN

"You are not broken. You are becoming."

Every woman carries a world within her.

A quiet world filled with stories.

Some joyful, some painful, some still unfolding.

This chapter isn't just about sharing my journey — it's about reminding you that your own story is powerful, even when it's messy, even when it's still healing.

Because every step you've taken has shaped the woman you're becoming.

Take a breath. Think back.

What moments have shaped you?

Inner Power: My Greatest Discovery

To me, inner power isn't about being the loudest voice in the room. It's that steady flame inside — the one that keeps burning even when life tries to blow it out. It's the part of you that whispers "Try again" when your heart is tired. I've seen it in myself. I've seen it in the women around me — my mother, my sister, my friends, my teachers. Some days it's buried, some days it's bold. But it's always there.

Reflect:

- When do you feel most in touch with your inner power?
- Who taught you, by example, what strength looks like?

Why I Wrote This Book

I wrote this for every woman who's ever felt invisible. For the girl who never felt seen. For the woman who is still learning to hear her own voice after years of being told to stay quiet.
I wrote this so that you don't just read about strength — you begin to feel it rising inside you.

Ask Yourself:

- When was the last time you felt unseen?
- What would it mean to be fully visible, even just to yourself?

A Life Full of Expectations — and a Decision to Rise

Growing up in a family of teachers, expectations were everywhere. My sister was brilliant, and when life didn't give her what she deserved, that pressure somehow passed on to me. I wasn't always a top student. But one day, I decided I wanted to change the story—not for anyone else, but because something inside me said, "You can." And I did. I topped my school. I met my strength for the first time.

Now You:

- What's one moment where you were surprised even by yourself?
- How did it feel to rise when no one expected you to?

The Decade of Searching

Between 14 and 24, I was chasing answers I couldn't name. I looked for happiness in achievements, identity in approval, and meaning in places that didn't fit me. But something shifted when I stopped looking outward and turned inward. I remembered the girl I used to be — playful, light-hearted, free. And in finding her, I began finding myself.

Gentle Prompt:

- Who were you before the world told you who to be?
- What parts of her still live inside you?

Resilience in Silence

There were moments when I felt undone. PMS overwhelmed me to the point of breaking. I cried, screamed, lashed out — and then asked myself, "Will this last forever?" And the truth was — it wouldn't. I began to trust that the storm would pass. I stopped fearing my emotions and started holding space for them.

Ask Yourself:

- What do you tend to resist in yourself, and what might happen if you let it in with compassion?
- When was the last time you reminded yourself: "This, too, shall pass"?

Healing in Layers

Healing doesn't happen all at once. Sometimes you think you're fine... and then a scent, a song, a memory pulls you back. That's okay. Healing is a spiral, not a straight line. I've learned to meet those moments with grace, not judgment. And that's made all the difference.

Reflection:

- What memory still stings — and what would it feel like to forgive yourself for still feeling it?
- What does healing mean to you today?

Failure — My Toughest Teacher

I used to think failure meant I wasn't good enough. Now I know it's where the most growth happens. Every failure taught me something success never could — humility, patience, self-trust. Failure shaped me far more than winning ever did.

Pause Here:

- What has failure taught you that you wouldn't trade?
- What did it lead you toward that you now cherish?

My Turning Point

There was a moment I realised: I don't owe anyone a version of myself that makes them comfortable. I stopped living to meet expectations and started living in alignment. And when I did that, my entire inner world shifted.

Prompt for You:

- Where in your life are you still trying to prove something, and to whom?
- What would change if you only needed your own approval?

Letting Go to Grow

I've let go of friendships, habits, thoughts, and pieces of myself. It's hard — but every time, I made space for something better. Peace became my new standard. If something disturbed that peace, it no longer had a place in my life.

Consider This:

- What have you outgrown, but are still holding onto out of habit or fear?
- What would you gain if you released it?

Misunderstood But Not Broken

People misunderstood my silence. They thought it meant weakness. But I've learned that silence can be sacred. It's where I meet my truth. I no longer feel the need to explain who I am. I just choose to be it.

Reflect:

- Has your silence ever been mistaken for weakness?
- What does silence give you that words cannot?

The Woman Society Didn't Expect

Society wanted me to be small, polite, agreeable, and obedient. But I chose to be honest, curious, and bold. I didn't want to fit the mould. I wanted to make my own. Not out of rebellion, but out of truth.

Now Ask Yourself:

- Where have you conformed just to feel accepted?
- What version of you is waiting to be expressed?

Redefining Strength

Strength isn't always loud. It's in the quiet courage to ask for help. To set a boundary. To start again. My strength is soft, steady, and deeply rooted. It doesn't always roar, but it never leaves.

Your Turn:

- How has your definition of strength evolved over the years?
- What does strength look like on you?

If My Younger Self Saw Me Now...

She would smile. She'd whisper, "I knew we'd get here." She'd see the woman I've become — not perfect, but whole. Not unscarred, but radiant. She'd see home in me. And she'd feel safe.

Close Your Eyes & Ask:

- What would your younger self say about who you are today?
- How can you honour her more often?

To Every Woman Reading This

You are not too sensitive, too emotional, too loud, too soft, too strong. You are exactly as you need to be. You

are not behind. You are becoming. Your pain holds power.
Your softness is sacred. And your journey — no matter how
messy — is worthy of love.

You are already a wonder.

Even if the world doesn't see it yet, you do.

And that's where it all begins.

THREE
Emotional Strength & Mental Health

Holding the Storm Inside

Emotional strength isn't about hiding your pain.

It's not about holding back tears, faking smiles, or pretending everything is fine.

To me, emotional strength is about showing up anyway. It's choosing direction over drift. Presence over numbness. Truth over silence.

It's the quiet decision to keep going — not perfectly, not always gracefully, but honestly.

I've cried.

Over exams. Rejections. Misunderstandings. Heartbreaks. But I always got back up — maybe not the next day, but eventually. That's a strength. Not the absence of pain, but the choice to move forward through it.

Pause and reflect:

- What does emotional strength look like in your life right now?
- When was the last time you surprised yourself by how well you held on?

I've learned to let myself feel deeply. I cry when I need to. I vent when it's necessary. I talk to people who listen with their hearts, not just their ears. Sometimes, I write down everything I'm feeling — not to fix it, but to release it. That, in itself, is healing.

Ask yourself:

- Do you give yourself permission to fall apart, just a little, without guilt?
- How do you process pain when it shows up?

There's a line that carried me through many breakdowns:
"This moment will change."
And it always does.

The Weight We Carry

As women, we're often told we feel too much. That we're too sensitive. Too dramatic. Too emotional.
But I see our emotions differently.
I see them as our strength, not something to hide, but something to honour.
Still, the emotional weight placed on us is real.
I wasn't just living for myself — I was living for the dreams others had handed down to me. I had to be the good girl. The achiever. The one who redeemed what was lost. There

was no room for mistakes. Even joy felt like a distraction I couldn't afford.

Reflect here:

- Whose expectations are you still carrying?
- Are there "shoulds" you've accepted that don't feel true to your soul?

Breaking Free

There were moments I felt gaslighted — not out of cruelty, but out of conditioning.
Indian families don't always mean to control, but they carry the weight of their own unhealed stories — fear, survival, sacrifice. I found myself trapped in their version of what was "good," "right," and "expected."
Eventually, I reached a point where staying quiet hurt more than speaking up.
Yes, I may have shouted. I may have been misunderstood.
But I did what I had to do: I made myself clear. I showed them I wasn't just a daughter or a mirror of their hopes — I was a whole person with my own voice, dreams, and path.

Ask yourself:

- Have you ever felt silenced or shaped by someone else's idea of who you should be?
- What would it feel like to finally say, "This is who I am"?

Healing the Mind and the Heart

These days, I feel safer within myself.
Not because everything is perfect — it never is.
But because I've built trust with my own heart.
I still have low moments. But I'm learning to meet them with patience, not panic. To say, "I see you. I'll sit with you. But I won't let you take over."
That's emotional strength. It's the ability to be your own safe place, even when the world isn't.

Reflect gently:

- Do you feel emotionally safe in your own mind and heart?
- What small acts of kindness could you offer yourself today?

To every woman reading this — to every person holding more than they show:
You are doing better than you think.
You are stronger than you feel.
You are allowed to fall apart and rebuild — as many times as it takes.
Let go of overthinking.
Hold onto hope.
Speak to the universe — or to your own heart — and ask for what you need.
Then trust: it's already on its way.

Journaling Prompts: Emotional Strength & Mental Health

- What does emotional strength mean to you, and how has your definition evolved?
- Think of a time you felt emotionally broken. What helped you rise again?
- Are there unspoken expectations that still shape your choices today?
- Have you ever ignored or suppressed your feelings to avoid conflict or judgment?
- What boundaries could protect your peace more fully?
- When life gets overwhelming, what affirmation or belief grounds you the most?
- What would your younger self need to hear in her most vulnerable moment?
- How can you show up for yourself more lovingly during emotional lows?
- What does self-kindness actually look like in your everyday life?

You don't have to carry everything all the time.
Let your tears fall when they need to. Let your voice rise when it must.
And above all, let your emotions guide you, not define you.
Because strength is not in how little you feel —
It's in how deeply you keep choosing to live.

FOUR

RECLAIMING VOICE & IDENTITY

Becoming Loud in a World That Silences

There was a time I stopped using my voice — not because I had nothing to say, but because it didn't feel like anyone wanted to hear it. Not really. My tears didn't invite comfort, only criticism. My silence didn't raise questions, only assumptions. And so, slowly, I hardened.

I wasn't cold. I was protecting myself.

I stopped crying in front of my family, not because I stopped feeling, but because my feelings weren't safe there. I became emotionally sharp, defensive. Not because I wanted to be, but because that's what survival looked like in a space where softness was never welcomed.

And still... I wonder.

If someone had just asked me, "What do you need right now?"

If someone had sat beside me, without fixing or judging,

just present —
Maybe I would've melted.
    But no one did.
So I learned to carry it quietly.
Maybe you have, too.

Pause and reflect:

- Can you remember a time when you felt unseen or emotionally shut down?
- How did you learn to protect yourself?

What Is Freedom, Really?

There came a point where I looked at the life I was living and asked, Whose version of 'good' is this?
Whose dreams am I carrying? Whose approval am I chasing?
I realized that true freedom isn't something that's handed to you — not by parents, not by relationships, not by society. It's something you claim. It's saying, "I choose to live in my truth, not in someone else's expectations."
To me, freedom is the ability to show up as your full self — wild, soft, spiritual, emotional, bold, loving, loud — and still feel worthy of space, respect, and belonging.

Ask yourself:

What does freedom look like for you — in your relationships, your choices, your expression?
Is it something you're living now... or still reaching for?

More Than Their Labels

I've been labelled.
Plump. Too sensitive. Too stubborn. Too ambitious. Too emotional.
Too much and not enough — all at the same time.
But here's what I've come to know:
Those labels were never mine.
They were someone else's projections, fears, and discomforts.
Because when a woman begins to know herself, to love herself, to own who she is, the world doesn't always know what to do with that.
But she does.

Now ask yourself:

- Have you ever been labelled in a way that made you feel small?
- Who are you beneath the labels?

Rebuilding Myself

Reclaiming my voice didn't happen overnight. It took time. It took inner conflict. It took breaking and rebuilding. I had to unlearn obedience. I had to question the stories I was raised with — stories that told me not to be "too loud," "too proud," "too emotional."
I had to teach myself to speak again — not in anger, but in truth.
Not to fight, but to be free.

Now, I use my voice with intention. I speak with clarity. I express emotions with grace, not aggression. I've learned that communicating doesn't mean overpowering — it means connecting.

And I don't explain myself to be accepted anymore.
I speak because my truth matters.

Reflect gently:

- Are there parts of you still afraid to be seen or heard?
- What would it feel like to express yourself without shrinking?

Speak. Scream. Sing. Just Don't Stay Silent.

To the woman still holding her voice inside
The one who's been told she's too emotional, too dramatic, too loud...
The one who's been quiet for too long...
You don't need permission to be fully yourself.
Speak, even if your voice shakes.
Cry, even if they call you weak.
Say what you need, even if it's not what they want to hear.
Because silence is not strength.
Expression is.
Clarity is.
Ownership is.
You were never meant to be invisible.
You were born to be heard.

Journal Prompts: Reclaiming Voice & Identity

- Can you recall a moment when you felt silenced? How did you respond, and what did you learn?
- Do you feel safe expressing your emotions with your family or loved ones? If not, what's missing?
- What labels have been placed on you, and how have they affected how you see yourself?
- What parts of your identity are you still hiding or healing?
- What would it feel like to release the expectations others placed on you?
- Are you clear on what you truly want, separate from what others want for you?
- How do you typically express your emotions, and what forms of expression feel most healing to you?
- What does it mean to you to "communicate with grace"? How would you like to grow in that area?
- What would you say to the version of yourself who once felt voiceless or invisible?
- What does she need to hear now, from you?

Let this chapter be your invitation back to your voice. Back to the version of you that was never too much, just too powerful to fit in a small life.
You don't need to shout to be strong.
You just need to speak in your own way, in your own time.
Because reclaiming your voice is not rebellion.
It's remembering who you are.

FIVE

SELF-LOVE & ACCEPTANCE

Learning to See Yourself Without Conditions

Self-love is not about vanity.

It's not about perfect skin, curated photos, or loud affirmations.

It's about looking into the mirror — tired eyes, messy hair, dark circles and all — and still whispering, "I'm enough."

It's about knowing that your worth isn't earned through approval, achievement, or appearance.

It lives within you, untouched, unchanging, and entirely yours.

I can't say I've mastered self-love.

But I'm learning. I'm trying.

And some days, that's enough.

Pause and reflect:

What does self-love look like for you today, not ideally, but honestly?

Are you still waiting for a version of yourself to "deserve" love?

The Mirror I Used to Avoid

There were days I hated how I looked.
My dark neck. My puffy face. My uneven skin. My crooked teeth.
I envied the girls who seemed effortlessly beautiful — glowing, confident, polished. I thought beauty belonged to them, and not to me.
Makeup never felt like magic. Confidence didn't come easily. I had to work for my peace, not just on the outside, but deep within. I found my glow through little acts of care: being kind to others, writing what I couldn't say aloud, listening to music that wrapped around me like warmth.
That was my healing.
Not cosmetics. Not compliments.
But connection to myself and to life.

Now ask yourself:

- What parts of your body or being have you struggled to accept?
- How do you care for yourself emotionally, especially when you feel low?

When I Feel Unlovable

There are days I wake up feeling empty.
Unattractive. Unmotivated. Disconnected from everything,

including myself.

But I remind myself: these are just clouds. They pass.
They don't define me.
They don't cancel out all the light I carry.

On those days, I search for something grounding — a conversation, a warm drink, a walk, a story about someone who's endured more than I can imagine. If they can survive, then so can I. If they can find light in darkness, maybe I can too.

Ask yourself gently:

- What helps you feel grounded when your self-worth feels shaky?
- Who or what reminds you that this moment isn't permanent?

The Comparison Trap

Comparison. Envy. Jealousy.
They all live in the same house. And sometimes, they try to rent space in mine.

Sure, I've wished for a better figure. Brighter skin. Sharper features. But I never truly wished to be anyone else. Why would I? Every woman is living her own unseen battle. No one's life is as effortless as it appears.

I can't live her story.
She can't live mine.
And beauty? Beauty without kindness is just decoration.

Reflect here:

- Who are you comparing yourself to — and what do you think they have that you don't?
- What would happen if you stopped measuring yourself against someone else's chapter?

How Loving Myself Changed Everything

When I started loving myself, even imperfectly, my relationships began to heal.
I showed up softer. I listened more. I reacted less.
I didn't love others from a place of needing to be loved back.
I loved it because I had love inside me, and it overflowed.

Self-love made me a better daughter. A better partner. A better friend.
Not perfect — but present.

Ask yourself:

- Has your relationship with yourself influenced the way you relate to others?
- What would it feel like to love others from a place of wholeness, not emptiness?

Staying True to Myself

Even when others upset me, I try not to change my core.
It's not always easy.
But when I imagine the person in front of me as a child, scared, learning, unsure, I soften.
That's not weakness.
That's a strength rooted in love.

And love, when you truly understand it, doesn't scream to be heard.
It stands still and shines.

Ask yourself:

- What parts of yourself do you protect the most when you feel hurt?
- What would it look like to respond with compassion toward others and yourself?

A Note to My Younger Self

If I could go back, I'd hold her hand.
I'd tell her:
"You are more lovable than you've ever been told.
You don't need to change your shape, your voice, your softness, your spark.
The right people will find you — but more importantly, you'll find yourself.
Keep your vision high, your heart kind, and your love rooted.
You don't need to prove anything. You just need to be you."

Now you:

- What would you say to your younger self in her most insecure moment?
- What does she need to hear from you today?

Self-love isn't a destination. It's a daily return.
To your truth.

To your softness.
To your power.
     And in that returning, you begin to glow.
From the inside out.
     Because when you love yourself, even just a little...
Everything begins to shift.

SIX

RELATIONSHIPS & BOUNDARIES

Loving Without Losing Yourself

Every woman knows what it's like to pour.
To give love before she's received it.
To stay when she's tired.
To keep the peace by sacrificing her own.

Relationships — whether with family, partners, friends, or community — shape our emotional world. They teach us love, loyalty, patience. But they can also teach us silence, guilt, and self-abandonment… if we're not careful.

This chapter isn't about walking away from love.
It's about returning to yourself within it.
It's about loving without losing your voice.
Caring without crossing your own limits.
Staying connected while staying whole.

Pause and reflect:

Do you ever feel like you're expected to give more than you can?

What would it mean to protect your peace — even in the relationships that matter most?

What Makes a Relationship Truly Healthy?

A healthy relationship isn't just built on love.
It's built on effort, respect, space, and communication.
And most of all — a willingness to try.

We often expect perfect understanding, but the truth is: no one can fully read our minds. Misunderstandings happen. Assumptions take over. But healing happens when both people want to understand — even if they fall short sometimes.

Ask yourself:

- Are your closest relationships built on trying, not just talking, but listening?
- Do you feel safe to be your full self, even when it's messy?

Boundaries: The Quiet Form of Power

Many women are raised to believe that setting boundaries is selfish. That saying no is rude. That protecting your energy makes you "too much" or "too distant."
But boundaries are not rejection — they are self-respect.
A boundary says:
"I love you — and I love me too."

It's not about keeping people out.
It's about knowing what gets to come in.

Reflect:

- Where in your life have you been told to "adjust" or "sacrifice" more than you could give?
- What boundary could you set today that would feel like a breath of fresh air?

When Boundaries Are Misunderstood

One of the hardest things is being misunderstood for doing what's best for you.

I've been told I only think about myself when I try to protect my space. But is caring for your own happiness really wrong?

No.

It's necessary.

Because if we keep overextending ourselves, we don't just lose energy — we lose clarity. And in that fog, we begin to forget our worth.

Now ask:

- Has someone ever made you feel guilty for choosing yourself?
- How can you stand in your truth without overexplaining it?

Self-Respect in Love

Love without respect is not love — it's dependency.
It's an obligation. It's exhaustion disguised as loyalty.

A woman deserves a love that sees her clearly, not for what she gives, but for who she is. She deserves to be accepted without needing to shrink. Honoured, not handled.

You don't have to chase someone to feel worthy.
You just have to remember that worthiness lives inside you, untouched.

Journal this:

- Do your relationships reflect your self-worth, or do they require you to earn it over and over again?
- What kind of love do you want to give yourself more consistently?

Walking Away From What No Longer Serves You

Letting go doesn't mean you didn't care.
It means you cared enough not to keep bleeding.

I've walked away from people I once trusted deeply — friends who used my loyalty, who drained my spirit. It hurt. But I didn't walk away because I stopped loving them.
I walked away because I finally started loving me.

Consider:
Who in your life drains more than they pour?

What would happen if you released loyalty to someone who no longer respects you?

Breaking the Guilt Cycle

For generations, women — especially our mothers — were praised for putting themselves last. Sacrifice was mistaken for love. Silence was mistaken for peace.

But we're not here to repeat that.

We're here to break cycles.

To show our daughters and sisters that it's okay to want more.

To model self-worth, not just survival.

Reflect here:

- What belief about being a "good woman" or "good daughter" are you ready to release?
- How can you model healthy boundaries without guilt?

Love Doesn't Mean Losing Yourself

You can care deeply and still have limits.

You can love fiercely and still need space.

You can give without giving yourself away.

Real strength is in balance — knowing when to nurture, and when to say enough.

Think about this:

- How do you balance love and assertiveness in your life?
- Where do you still hold back out of fear of being "too much"?

A Love Letter to Every Woman Holding It All Together

Speak.
Ask.
Set the line.
Reclaim the space.
You are allowed to take up room in your home, your relationships, and your world.
You are allowed to protect your peace.
And you never have to feel guilty for needing time, rest, distance, or truth.
Because love should never cost you your voice.
Respect should never ask you to vanish.
You don't have to give endlessly to be good.
You just have to be whole to be enough.

SEVEN
COURAGE & CONFIDENCE

The Quiet Power You Carry

Courage and confidence don't always shout.

Sometimes, they whisper.

They show up in the decisions no one sees — the quiet "yes" to yourself, the brave "no" when something doesn't feel right, the moments you keep going when everything in you wants to stop.

For women, courage isn't just a trait. It's a lifeline.

And confidence? It becomes the armor we build — not to hide who we are, but to protect the woman we're becoming.

We live in a world that underestimates our strength.

But we don't need the world to see it.

We just need to feel it within ourselves.

Pause and reflect:

- What does courage feel like in your body — steady, shaky, bold, or quiet?

- When was the last time you surprised yourself with your own strength?

What Courage Really Is

To me, courage is the ability to feel fear and still move forward.
Not because you're fearless, but because you've decided that your purpose matters more than your fear.
As women, courage becomes our daily companion.
It's in walking home late at night.
It's in speaking up in a room where we were taught to stay quiet.
It's in pursuing dreams that don't fit the mold.
Courage isn't loud.
It's consistent.

Ask yourself:

- When was the last time you chose courage over comfort?
- What fear are you carrying right now — and what would happen if you faced it?

A Rainy Night: Proof of Power

I remember a night when I had to travel alone, late, in the rain, through unfamiliar roads. Everything about the moment told me to panic. But I didn't. I stayed steady. I got home safely.

To someone else, it might seem small.
But to me, it was proof.
Proof that courage doesn't wait for applause.
It simply acts when needed.

You have moments like that too — moments that proved you were braver than you believed.

Reflect gently:

- What small act of courage have you overlooked in your own story?
- How might your life change if you gave yourself credit for it?

Confidence: Built From Within

Confidence isn't about having all the answers.
It's about trusting yourself to figure it out — even if you fail, even if it's messy.

What gives me confidence is simple: I know who I am.
I know how many times I've fallen and stood back up.
I've said no when it wasn't easy. I've chosen myself even when it meant losing people.
And that's where confidence is born — in the quiet clarity of knowing your own truth.

Ask yourself:

- What decision have you made recently that made you feel proud, even if no one else noticed?
- What does confidence mean to you, beyond appearance?

Handling Doubt & Criticism

People will always have opinions.
They will doubt you without knowing your story.
They'll project their own fears onto your courage.
But I've learned not to give their voices more weight than my own.
They didn't live my life.
They didn't carry my battles.
So why should they decide my worth?
That mindset took time. It took practice.
But it changed everything.

Now you:

- Who are you still trying to prove yourself to — and why?
- What would happen if you stopped needing external approval?

If You're Struggling With Confidence...

Let me tell you this — your spark is still there.
Even if life dimmed it. Even if others couldn't see it.
You don't have to wait years.
Sometimes, all it takes is one decision to believe in yourself.
One moment of saying: I choose me.
That's how it begins.

Say this softly:

- "I don't have to be perfect to be powerful. I just have to show up."

7 Steps to Build Courage & Confidence

1. **Start with small risks**. Speak up. Say no. Try something new. Let courage stretch you slowly.
2. **Keep promises to yourself**. Your self-trust grows when you follow through — even on the little things.
3. **Celebrate tiny wins**. Notice them. Name them. "I did that," even if it's just getting out of bed.
4. **Talk to yourself like someone you love.** Your inner voice matters more than anyone else's. Let it be kind.
5. **Surround yourself with soul-nourishing people**. Uplifting energy creates a safe place to grow.
6. **Reflect regularly**. Ask, "When did I feel brave this week?" Let your courage be visible to you.
7. **Embrace discomfor**t. Fear doesn't mean stop. It often means you're growing. Let discomfort be a teacher.

Journal with this:

- What's one small risk you can take this week?
- How can you speak to yourself with more encouragement and softness?

You already have everything you need to be courageous. You've already survived things that once felt impossible. So don't wait for the world to crown you with confidence.

Crown yourself — today, now, exactly as you are.

Because courage is not about never being afraid.
It's about moving forward, even when you are.

EIGHT

SACRED SISTERHOOD — THE POWER OF FEMALE FRIENDSHIPS

Why Every Woman Needs Another Woman in Her Lifetime

Some women enter your life like sunlight — not loud, not dramatic… just warm, steady, and healing.

They don't try to fix you. They simply sit beside you in your silence, when words are too heavy and your heart too tired. They hold your truth when you've forgotten it. They say, "You don't have to be strong today. I've got you."

These are not just friendships. They are lifelines. Soul contracts. Sacred bonds.

And every woman needs at least one.

Because there are certain things only another woman truly understands — the weight of expectations, the ache of being too much or not enough, the pressure to care for everyone else while ignoring your own needs.

Another woman knows what it means to show up bleeding — emotionally or otherwise — and still smile. Still serve. Still survive.

And when you're seen by another woman who understands this?

It feels like coming home.

What Female Friendships Have Taught Me

They've taught me that love doesn't need to be earned. That you can laugh even while you're breaking. That you can be held without being fixed. That you can grow in completely different directions and still be rooted in the same kind of love.

They've shown me I don't need a hundred people. Just one who sees me — really sees me — is enough to keep me anchored.

Reflect gently:

- Who is one woman in your life who has seen you without judgment?
- What have you learned from the women who've stood beside you?

When Friendships Break

Not all friendships are forever.

Some drift quietly. Others end with words you can't take back.

Some break your heart in a way even romance never did.

And it hurts deeply.

But letting go doesn't mean you failed.

It simply means the connection has run its course. You can love someone and still release them. You can miss the memories and still protect your peace. Growth isn't just about rising — it's about recognizing when something is no longer serving you.

Ask yourself:

- Have you outgrown a friendship recently? What did it teach you?
- Can you hold gratitude for what it gave you without needing to keep it?

The Types of Friends That Are Pure Gold

Some friendships change you forever. Some walk beside you for a season. And some — they're your mirror, your anchor, your fire, your soul.

The Mirror: She reflects your best self back to you — even when you've forgotten who you are.

The Anchor: She grounds you. You can fall apart with her, and she still shows up steady.

The Firestarter: She challenges you to grow. She's the one pushing you to take the risk, say the truth, be bold.

The Soul Sister: She just knows. Words aren't always needed. Her presence is enough.

Reflect here:

· Which type of friend are you to the women in your life?
· Which type are you still seeking?

If You're Feeling Lonely Right Now...

You are not broken. You are not unworthy.
You are in a season of shedding.

Sometimes, the loneliness you feel is simply space being cleared for the right women to enter. The ones who will meet you where you are — not where you pretend to be.

In the meantime, be your own best friend.
Take yourself out. Write yourself love notes. Remind yourself that the first woman you need to trust, to care for, and to be kind to... is you.

Pause and ask:

· Are you being the kind of friend you want to attract?
· How can you hold space for yourself the way you hold it for others?

Why Every Woman Needs Another Woman

We heal through each other.
There are wounds therapy can touch — and there are wounds only a woman's gentle "Me too" can soften.

We need each other to remind us:
That we are not crazy — we are growing.

That softness is strength.
That we can rise without stepping on one another.
That we can be mirrors, not comparisons. Reflections, not rivals.

The right woman won't compete with you. She'll fix your crown when it slips.
She'll speak your name with honour in rooms where you're not present.
She'll call you out with love, not to shame you, but to free you.

In a world that often tries to turn women against each other, choose the ones who lift you. And more importantly, be that woman.

Take a moment:

- What would it mean for you to show up for another woman, not just when it's easy, but when it matters?
- What's one friendship you want to nurture more intentionally?

Final Reflections — On Sisterhood & Letting Go

- Who in your life truly sees you, and how does that feel?
- What kind of friend do you want to be — not just for others, but for yourself?
- Write a letter to a friend (past or present) you've never fully expressed yourself to. What do you need to say?
- What do you wish more women believed about female friendship?

Final Words: Let Friendship Be Sacred

Celebrate the women who show up.
Who checks on you when no one else does?
Who remembers your coffee order?
Who sits in silence when there are no words?
Who doesn't need you to be perfect, just real?
And if you haven't found them yet, don't worry.
You're still becoming the version of yourself who will draw them in.
Let friendship be soft. Let it be sacred.
Let it be the safe place we've all been waiting for.

NINE

BREAKING GENERATIONAL PATTERNS

The Brave Work of Becoming

"You weren't born to repeat — you were born to rewrite."

Some women are born into love.

Some into silence.

Some into sacrifice.

But some — like you — are born to break the pattern.

Not out of rebellion.

Out of truth.

Because your spirit knows: you weren't made to carry pain that didn't start with you.

You were made to end it.

The Invisible Inheritance

Sometimes we inherit more than eye colour or family recipes.

We inherit shame.
We inherit silence.
   "Be the good girl."
"Don't ask for too much."
"Be grateful, even when it hurts."
"Family comes first, even at your own cost."

These phrases aren't just culture — they are emotional chains. They wrap around generations of women and whisper that suffering is noble. But you, dear one, were not born to live like that.

You were born to set yourself — and others — free.

Reflect gently:

- What emotional rules were passed down to you, silently or loudly?
- Which ones are you ready to unlearn?

My Realization

I remember the moment I questioned my role, not just as a daughter or a sister, but as a woman.
I watched my mother give and give, until there was nothing left for herself.
I watched her apologise for needing rest, for asking for space, for wanting more.

And I whispered quietly to myself: *This will not be my story.*

I didn't know what freedom looked like yet. But I knew what it didn't feel like.
And so I began to seek — even if that meant being misunderstood by the people I loved most.

Ask yourself:

- Has anyone in your family ever modelled joy, rest, or boundary-setting?
- What version of womanhood were you expected to repeat?

The Guilt of Choosing Yourself

The first time you say "no"...
The first time you speak your truth...
The first time you set a boundary...
It might sting.
It might feel like betrayal.
Because we were taught that love equals sacrifice.
That pleasing others is more noble than honouring ourselves.
But choosing yourself is not betrayal.
It's healing.
It's how the cycle breaks.

Now pause and ask:

- What does guilt whisper when you start choosing yourself?
- What would love — real love — whisper instead?

Becoming the First

You might be the first in your family to do the hard work.

The first to go to therapy.
The first to name trauma.
The first to raise a child with emotional freedom.
The first to stop normalising burnout, silence, or shame.
The first to parent yourself with compassion when no one else did.

And it may feel lonely at times.
But it's also holy.

Because you're not just healing yourself — you're healing forward and backwards, across generations.

Reflect here:

- What are you doing now that no one before you dared to do?
- How does it feel to be the first?

A Passage for the Cycle-Breaker

There is a quiet kind of courage in the woman who decides to end the pattern.
She may be the first to rest without guilt.
The first to cry without shame.
The first to choose joy without permission.

She's not louder than others — just more awake.
She stops carrying things that don't belong to her.
She stops shrinking to protect others' comfort.
She starts becoming the woman her mother never had the chance to be — softer, freer, more whole.

She doesn't need the world's permission.
She doesn't need validation.

She's rewriting the story not just for herself,
but for every daughter, niece, sister, and future soul who
will rise from her healing.

Reflection Prompts: Are You the Cycle-Breaker?

- What beliefs or patterns did you inherit that no longer
serve you?
- Who in your family modelled sacrifice or silence, and
how did that shape you?
- Are you the first to define what "freedom" means in your
lineage?
- What is one rule or story you're ready to rewrite today?
- If you could speak to your mother's inner child, what
would you say to her?

Final Love Note to the Brave Ones

To the woman who is healing what her ancestors
couldn't...
To the one crying in secret because her path looks so
different...
To the one daring to live, love, and lead from truth instead
of trauma...
You are not selfish.
You are sacred.
You are not too much.
You are just enough to end what should've ended long ago.
And when your daughter — or your inner child — looks
up and asks,
"How did you do it?"

You'll smile and say:
"I remembered who I was. And I chose to become free."

TEN

CREATIVITY AS HEALING

Finding Yourself Through Expression

Creativity isn't just something you do.

It's something that lives in you.

It's how your soul speaks when your voice feels tired.

It's how pain becomes poetry. How silence becomes a song. How confusion turns into color.

For so many women, creativity has always existed — quietly, instinctively, almost invisibly.

We doodled in notebooks during math class.

We hummed while folding clothes.

We danced barefoot in our rooms when no one was watching.

We scribbled secrets into diaries after heartbreak.

And in those moments, something inside us whispered: Let it out.

And when we do... something softens.

A weight is lifted. The chaos inside finds a rhythm.

That's the power of expression.

That's the beginning of healing.

Why Expression Matters

We're not always taught how to express ourselves, especially as women.
Sometimes, we're silenced by family.
Sometimes by fear.
Sometimes, by the quiet belief that we're "not good enough" to create anything worth sharing.
But expression was never about being good.
It's about being real.
You don't need to be a painter to make art.
You don't need to be a writer to write something that heals you.
You don't need talent — just truth.
When we express, we process.
We release.
We reclaim the parts of ourselves that we buried to survive.

Ask yourself:

- Have you ever judged your creativity before you even let it live?
- What would it feel like to create without needing it to be "good"?

My Creative Healing

There were times I couldn't say what I felt, so I wrote it.
When I felt too heavy to speak, I let music hold me.
When I didn't have answers, I colored the confusion.

When I felt lost, I created small, quiet things — not to be seen, but to find myself again.

My creativity has never lived on stages or gallery walls. It has lived in corners. In journals. In half-finished poems. In broken, beautiful sentences.

And that was enough.

It still is.

Because I don't create to be impressive.

I create to feel whole.

Reflect gently:

- When was the last time you made something — just for yourself?
- What did it feel like to express, even if no one else ever saw it?

Ways to Heal Through Creativity

There's no "right" way to be creative.

There's only your way.

Here are a few gentle paths you can explore:

- **Journaling** — Write freely, without editing. Let your thoughts pour out like water. Don't aim for sense. Aim for honesty.
- **Music** — Sing, hum, or just listen to what stirs your spirit. Let sound hold your emotions.
- **Movement** — Dance in your kitchen. Stretch in silence. Let your body speak without needing words.
- **Colour** — Doodle. Paint. Sketch what you feel. It doesn't have to be pretty. It just has to be yours.

- **Photography or Collage** — Capture the world around you. Build vision boards. Use imagery to mirror your inner world.

Creativity is where emotion becomes form.
Where something stuck inside finally finds a way out.

Ask yourself:

- What form of creativity feels safest for you to explore today?
- Which emotion needs expression right now?

If You've Forgotten Your Creative Self

Maybe someone once told you your art was silly.
Maybe life became too busy.
Maybe responsibilities buried your spark.
But she's still there — the little girl who used to make up stories in her head...
who sang to herself in front of the mirror...
who painted rainbows on walls and called them masterpieces.
She hasn't left.
She's waiting for you to invite her back.
You don't have to be confident.
You just have to be willing.
Let yourself create — badly, beautifully, boldly.
Not because you have something to prove.
But because you have something to feel.

Reflect here:

- What creative outlet did you love as a child? Can you bring it back, just for a day?
- If your inner artist could speak, what would she ask of you?

• 57 •

Final Thoughts: There Is Healing in Your Hands

You are not just here to work, think, or do.
You are here to create.
Your emotions deserve to be expressed.
Your silence deserves to be turned into sound.
Your story deserves to take shape — in colour, in words, in movement, in anything that feels like you.
There is healing in your hands.
In your voice.
In your breath.
You just have to give it a place to live.
And when you do — when you stop creating to be seen and start creating to see yourself —
that is when true healing begins.

ELEVEN

DAILY WONDER WOMAN RITUALS

Living with Intention, Power & Peace

Power doesn't always come with a bang.

Sometimes, it arrives softly — in the quiet rituals we return to when no one is watching.

In the way we speak to ourselves in the mirror.

In the way we care for our bodies.

In how we protect our peace, even from the inside out.

Being a Wonder Woman is not about doing it all or doing it perfectly.

It's not about checking every box or having your life figured out.

It's about intention.

It's about waking up and saying, "I will treat myself like I matter today."

Because you do.

And that one choice changes everything.

Why Rituals Matter

Routines are tasks.
Rituals are sacred.
They are small, repeatable acts that ground you, soften you, and return you to your centre.

On days when life is chaotic, when you're being pulled in too many directions, rituals don't just organise your time — they anchor your soul.

You don't need an hour.
You don't need perfection.
You just need presence.
Even five minutes, done with love, can reconnect you to your power.

Pause and ask yourself:

- What's one small moment you could reclaim for yourself each day?
- What would change if you treated that moment like something sacred?

Daily Practices That Hold You

You don't need a full routine to begin. You just need to return to yourself.
Here are a few grounding rituals that remind me of who I am, even when life feels like too much:

- **Morning Stillness** — Before the world gets loud, sit in silence. Breathe. Ask yourself, "What do I need today?"
- **Mirror Talk** — Look into your own eyes. Say something kind. Even if it feels awkward. Especially then.

- **Gratitude Notes** — Write down three things you're thankful for. They don't have to be big. Gratitude shifts everything.
- **Protective Boundaries** — Decide what energy is allowed near you today, and what isn't. Your peace is your home.
- **Evening Release** — Journal your day. What drained you? What lifted you? Let it out so you don't carry it into sleep.

These are not about doing more.
They're about feeling more connected to yourself.

Reflect here:

- What part of your day could become more intentional with just a little attention?
- What do you do each day that already feels like a ritual, even if you never called it that before?

Personal Anchors I Return To

There are days I feel lost, unmotivated, and overwhelmed.
But I've learned: I don't need to feel "in control" to be okay.
I just need to return to the small, sacred things that never fail me.

- Drinking water slowly, like it's holy.
- Making my bed like I'm creating peace in the world.
- Saying "no" when my body says "enough."
- Lighting a candle and watching it flicker like it's my soul speaking.

- Praying or meditating — not to ask for miracles, but to sit with strength.

These things don't fix me.
They honor me.
And that is enough.

Now you:

- What acts — no matter how small — help you feel rooted and real?
- Can you give yourself permission to come back to them, again and again?

Reflection Prompts: Rituals & Inner Power

- What daily habits drain you, and what would it feel like to release them?
- What is one thing you could do each day to feel more grounded or seen?
- When do you feel most connected to your strength — morning, night, after movement, after silence?
- What kind of words do you wish someone would say to you daily? Can you offer them to yourself?
- What does a "day of peace" actually look and feel like for you?

Final Thoughts

You don't need a 5 a.m. wake-up, green juice, and an hour of meditation to be powerful.

You just need to show up for yourself.

Consistently.

Gently.

Honestly.

Rituals are not chores. They are reminders.

That you matter.

That your energy is sacred.

Your life doesn't have to be a performance.

Let it be a prayer.

Let it be a collection of intentional, loving moments.

Because that's where real power lives.

In the spaces you reclaim for yourself, one breath, one boundary, one quiet moment at a time.

TWELVE
SPIRITUALITY & SELF-AWARENESS

Living in Harmony With the Universe and Your Inner Self

Spirituality isn't loud.

It's not about grand rituals or public displays of devotion.
It's quiet, powerful, and deeply personal — a connection between your soul, the universe, and your higher purpose.

To me, spirituality is about alignment.

When we live from our true essence — with clarity, kindness, and conscious presence — we don't just find peace... we become peace.

We radiate it.

We bring light into rooms that have forgotten what warmth feels like.

Why Spirituality Matters

Spirituality grounds us when life feels unsteady.
It reminds us that we are not alone. That there's a force greater than fear. That we can trust life, not because it's always easy, but because it always teaches.

My own spiritual practices — prayer, journaling, stillness, and manifestation — have taught me one powerful truth:
When you trust fully, life aligns.

You may not always get what you expect.
But you will always receive what you need.

Ask yourself gently:

- What does "being spiritually connected" feel like to you — calm, hopeful, clear?
- Where do you find the most clarity: stillness, nature, prayer, journaling, or somewhere else?

The Power of Trust

When you let go of doubt and surrender to what's meant for you, the universe starts to respond. It might not come the way you imagined — but it comes. Always.

There's a kind of magic that begins when you start thinking not about what can go wrong, but what can go right. When your thoughts shift from fear to faith, your entire reality begins to shift, too.

Reflection:

- What thoughts do you feed most often: possibility or worry?

- What would it feel like to focus only on what you want, as if it's already yours?

My Anchor in Storms

I've had moments of deep doubt. Moments when the path felt invisible, when nothing made sense, and hope felt like a distant memory.

But in those moments, I turn to nature.
To the rhythm of trees swaying.
To the stillness of stars.
To the flow of water that keeps moving, even when rocks try to stop it.

Nature reminds me that there's a season for everything — that nothing stays still forever.
And that even when life feels like a storm, the sky eventually clears.

Ask yourself:

- When you feel disconnected from yourself, where do you go to remember?
- What has nature taught you about resilience, softness, or change?

The Heart of Manifestation

Manifestation isn't about wishing — it's about believing.
It's not magic. It's alignment.
The universe doesn't respond to desperation — it responds to clarity, to intention, to energy.

The key isn't to ask for more. It's to act and feel as though it's already yours.

Speak in the language of already.

Trust that what is meant for you is already on its way.

And while you wait?

Live. Love. Give. Rest.

Let faith replace fear.

Gentle prompt:

- What desire have you been hesitant to claim because you don't yet believe you deserve it?
- Can you name one thing you're ready to fully trust is coming to you?

A Practice: The Path to Manifestation

Let's walk through a simple practice — a reflection path built on five steps. Each step helps you tune into your desires, align your energy, and deepen your trust.

Step 1: What do you truly desire?
A) To manifest happiness and peace
B) To receive validation from others

Step 2: What do you choose to focus on?
A) The potential and possibilities
B) The obstacles and "what-ifs"

Step 3: How do you trust the universe?
A) By letting go of doubt and surrendering to the process
B) By worrying about what may go wrong

Step 4: When life feels overwhelming, how do you respond?
A) Turn to nature, breath, or stillness for peace
B) Push harder, ignoring your emotions

Step 5: What truth will guide your journey?
A) The universe listens to your intentions; believe in yourself
B) Your worth depends on others' approval

If you chose mostly **A**, you're already walking in alignment. If you choose some **B**'s, let them show you where fear still holds your trust. No judgment — only awareness. You can always shift.

Final Reflections: The Soul's Truth

Spirituality is not about perfection. It's about presence. It's about showing up in the world as your real self—even when that self feels messy, unsure, or in progress.

It's about knowing that every experience — the pain, the confusion, the joy — is part of your soul's becoming.

So the next time you feel small, scared, or stuck, remember:
You are not lost.
You are being led.

Final Message: Trust the Plan

The universe listens.
To your energy.
To your thoughts.

To your quiet prayers spoken in the dark.
     Stay kind. Stay patient. Stay grounded in who you are.
Live from love — and everything else will align.
     Your life is not random.
It is a sacred unfolding.
Let it happen. Let it lead you. Let it change you.
     Because the universe is always on your side.
And your soul already knows the way.

THIRTEEN

DREAMS & PURPOSE

"A dream is the voice of your soul calling you to step into your greatness."

Dreams aren't just fleeting wishes—they are sacred seeds we plant with love and determination. A dream is something we're born to create, deeply tied to our life's purpose. Anyone can have dreams, but only those who stay consistent and passionate enough will see those dreams blossom into reality.

Reflection Prompt:

Think about a dream you've been holding onto for a while. What is one action you can take today to move toward it?

"The size of your dream doesn't matter. What matters is the size of your belief in it."

Distractions come and go like passing clouds, but the dream that truly belongs to you pulls you upward. I carry many dreams within me, and I'm working toward them without doubt or fear. My guiding mantra is simple, yet powerful: Nothing is impossible.

Engagement Point:

Pause for a moment and close your eyes. Imagine that the version of you who has already achieved her dreams is standing right in front of you. What does she say to you? How does she inspire you to take the next step?

"There are no limits to what you can achieve when you believe that nothing is impossible."

Sometimes, it's a person, a moment, or that quiet inner voice that speaks to you each morning—telling you to rise and try again. That voice is your fuel. It's the fire that keeps burning even when everything else seems dim.

Reflection Prompt:

Think of a time when that inner voice guided you through a challenge. How can you tune in to it more frequently?

"A dream isn't just a wish; it's a call to action."

There's a difference between struggling for a dream and joyfully working toward it. When you walk the path with happiness—even with all the ups and downs—it becomes easier, lighter, and more fulfilling.

"The joy of the journey is what makes the dream worth chasing."

I absolutely believe that every woman has her unique purpose in life. If you're still finding yours, don't worry—it's already within you, waiting to be heard.

Engagement Point:

What's one thing you've always dreamed of doing but have

been too afraid to try? What would it look like if you took the first step toward that dream today?

Activity: Puzzle of Purpose

Let's play a word scramble to remind yourself of your power! Unscramble the words and reflect on what each one means to you:

- MREADS → ________
- PSORUPE → ________
- FIATLH → ________
- ILBEVE → ________
- RWOMEON → ________

"Your power is in the words you speak to yourself."

Bonus Reflection: Pick one word from above and write a short affirmation using it. For example, "I believe in my purpose." How does this affirmation feel when you speak it aloud?

Closing Reflection

As you reach the end of this journey, remember that you are not simply closing a book—you are opening a new chapter in your life. The insights, reflections, and shifts you've experienced are not meant to stay contained within these pages. They are the beginning of a powerful transformation that has been waiting for you all along.

You have the power to dream boldly, to break cycles that no longer serve you, and to claim the purpose that has always been yours. The journey of becoming is ongoing, and while it may be challenging at times, it is also the most beautiful, freeing, and rewarding path you'll ever walk.

Take a moment to honor how far you've come. The woman you were yesterday and the woman you are today are not the same. You've taken steps toward healing, toward clarity, and toward embracing your inner power. That alone is something to celebrate.

Reflection Prompt:

Looking back on your journey through this book, what is the one shift or realization that stands out the most to you? How will you carry that forward into your everyday life?

Remember, the voice inside you—the one that whispered to you to rise, to keep going, to be brave—is your most faithful guide. Trust it. The world needs the full expression of who you are—there is no one like you, and your unique light is meant to shine brightly.

As you move forward, remember this:

"You are not just the dreamer of your story; you are the author, the creator, and the hero. Your power lies in your ability to rewrite your narrative, one choice at a time."

Keep rewriting. Keep dreaming. And most of all, keep choosing YOU.

With love and courage,
You are already everything you need to be.

Warm regards,
Saalini Vellivel